Atlantic Trade

and

Richard Oswald

improbablevoices.com

Understanding Eighteenth Century Atlantic Trade from the Unusual Perspective of Richard Oswald

Derek Dwight Anderson

Copyright ©2022 Derek Dwight Anderson
All Rights Reserved.

No part of this book may be reproduced or transmitted in any form or by any means, electronic or mechanical, including photocopying, recording, or by any information storage and retrieval system without permission in writing from the author.

ISBN-13: 9798359124102

Cover illustration: Pierre Charles Canot, 1710-1777, "A View of Charles Town the Capital of South Carolina in North America / Vue de Charles Town capitale de la Carolina du Sud dans l'Amérique Septentrionale," courtesy of Library of Congress, 2004672416.

Cataloging Data

Understanding Eighteenth Century Atlantic Trade from the Unusual Perspective of Richard Oswald /
Derek Dwight Anderson

Sausalito, California

Includes bibliographic references.
Series: Understanding World History Through Biography

1. Oswald, Richard, 1705-1784. 2. Slave trade. 3. Sugar trade. 4. Atlantic Ocean Region--Commerce

382.44092—dc23
LCC HF3025

**For additional resources and information visit:
improbablevoices.com**

PREFACE

I remain proud of the 2020 publication of *Improbable Voices: A History of the World Since 1450 Seen from Twenty-Six Unusual Perspectives*, but with the passage of time, I have come to appreciate the fact its length was unwieldy for certain readers. In an effort to make the work more accessible to those who are interested in specific eras, what I consider to be some of the best chapters of *Improbable Voices* are now being published individually. The result is more than a typical introduction to a topic, but this book will not be mistaken by experts as being a comprehensive or definitive work either. Instead, my hope is that motivated students, thoughtful instructors, and general readers who are looking for particular historical case studies will find the books in my Understanding World History Through Biography series to be a useful alternative to other available works.

As was true with *Improbable Voices* as a whole, my goal here is to try to explain an important moment in modern history and to celebrate biography as a genre without focusing upon well-known personalities. This is because lesser-known individuals also shape history just as history shapes people. My overall aim is to provide the reader with sufficient depth to gain an understanding of a life in the context of a particular time and to understand a given era through the experiences of a specific individual.

I retain my indebtedness to dozens of libraries and a multitude of individuals who supported me through the eight-year research, writing and publishing processes. Similarly, I remain steadfast in my dedication: "in honor of my students and great teachers—especially, Marty, Terry, and Valerie."

Words with an asterisk (*) are defined in the glossary on page 39.

Atlantic Trade and Richard Oswald

On November 21, 1741, a soap boiler named Samuel Lucas entered Thomas Dickenson's grocery store in Worcester, England and purchased two pounds of a high-quality hyson tea. As the grocer weighed and packaged the bulk green tea leaves from China for Lucas, it is doubtful either man thought about what was involved in bringing that tea to Worcester.[1] In all likelihood, they were simply focused upon the immediate transaction. Similarly, when the British earl Horace Walpole joined two thousand other ticket holders in London's Ranelagh Gardens in early May 1749 to commemorate the end of the War of the Austrian Succession,* his attention was not on how the booths serving tea with milk and sugar obtained their merchandise.[2] Instead, Walpole's focus was on the bands playing French horns, the troops of harlequin actors, the people dancing around a maypole, the gondolas adorned with flags and streamers that plied the canal, and the illuminated orange trees around the amphitheater.[3] He concentrated on the aesthetics, not the logistics. In fact, while most people in eighteenth century Britain didn't realize the enormous complexities involved in bringing sugar and tea to a grocery store or a garden party, there were those like global merchant Richard Oswald who most certainly did.

Oswald was born in 1705, two years before the Act of Union brought England and Scotland formally together as the United Kingdom of Great Britain.[4] He spent his boyhood in Caithness, mainland Britain's most northerly and quite impoverished shire, where his father was the Presbyterian minister in the coastal village of Dunnet. Like other children in the village, Oswald learned to read and write in a makeshift classroom underneath the steeple of his father's church since

---

[1] Jon Stobart, *Sugar and Spice: Grocers and Groceries in Provincial England 1650-1830* (Oxford, U.K.: Oxford University Press, 2013), 142, 195.
[2] By the 1720s, the manner in which the British drank tea had changed. It was no longer drunk plain, as in China, or as it had been when tea was first introduced to Europe. Instead, sugar and tea went hand-in-hand for the British of all social classes. See Woodruff D. Smith, "Complications of the Commonplace: Tea, Sugar, and Imperialism," *Journal of Interdisciplinary History*, 23, 2 (Autumn, 1992), 259-279, EBSCOhost.
[3] Horace Walpole, "To Mann, Wednesday 3 May, 1749 OS," *The Yale Edition of Horace Walpole's Correspondence, Volume 20: Horace Walpole's Correspondence with Sir Horace Mann IV*, W.S. Lewis, Warren Hunting Smith and George L. Lam (eds.) (New Haven, Connecticut: Yale University Press, 1960), 46.
[4] Most surviving records list Oswald's birth year as 1705, but his tombstone says he was born in 1700. See David Hancock, *Citizens of the World: London Merchants and the Integration of the British Atlantic Community, 1735-1785* (New York: Cambridge University Press, 1995), 61.

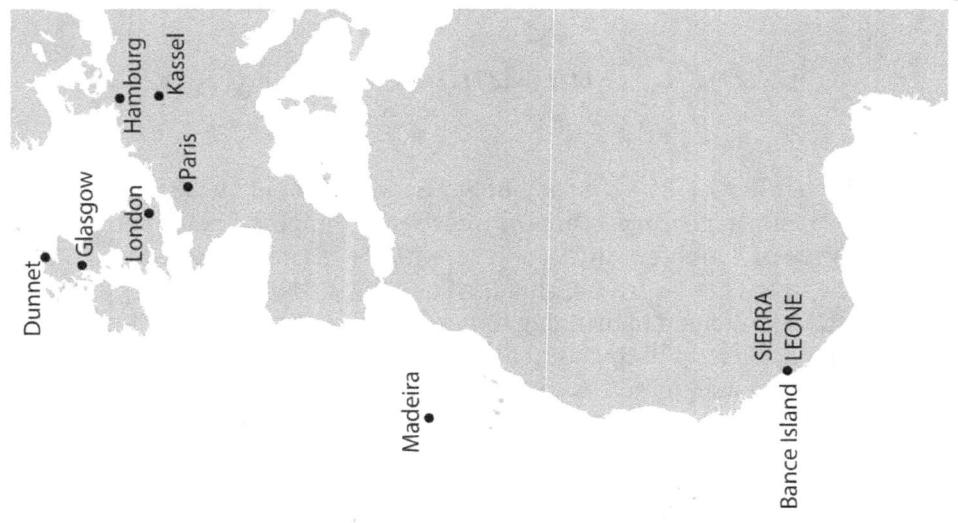
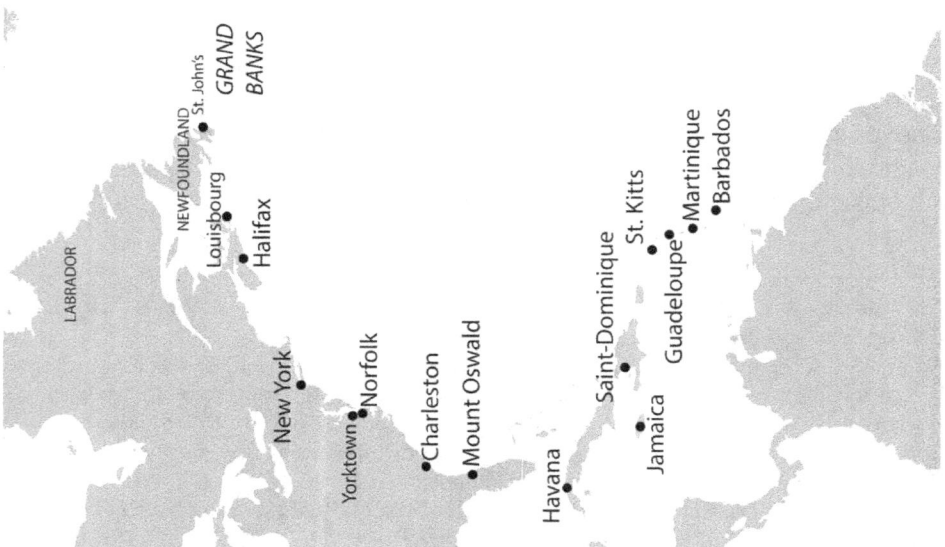

Figure 1: Map of the Atlantic World by Derek Dwight Anderson.

the nearest statutory school was impracticably far away.[5] At the age of twenty, Oswald heeded the call of urban life that so many rural youths hear. He moved to Glasgow to work as a clerk in the successful import-export business of his two older cousins. Their firm specialized in Virginia tobacco and the Oswalds were successful and prominent: by 1731 their company had become the fifth largest tobacco firm in the city, importing more than 300,000 pounds of the Chesapeake leaf a year.[6] By helping to keep the firm's records in an office overlooking Glasgow's Old Green, the younger Oswald began to develop his commercial acumen. In fact, he must have been a quick study because in the 1730s Oswald's cousins entrusted him to manage their operations on the American side of the Atlantic.

Oswald spent most of his six years in the Americas in Norfolk, Virginia. He arrived about the time the town received its 1736 charter of incorporation, which came as recognition of the port's growing commercial importance. Highlighted by a few two-story buildings, a courthouse, an Anglican church, and many taverns, Norfolk stood as an *entrepôt* for Tidewater planters, especially as the increased size of ocean-going vessels limited the number that could sail throughout Chesapeake Bay's estuaries. While the port also shipped grain, salted meat, timber, and animal skins, Norfolk's primary export was tobacco, and Glasgow became that commodity's primary destination.[7] As his cousins' agent in America, Oswald was responsible for both selling supplies to planters and for negotiating the purchase price for their crop.[8] His task was facilitated by the fact that tobacco growing had evolved into a carefully regulated industry in the colony. In 1730, the Virginia Assembly began requiring government inspection of all tobacco shipments prior to export.[9] According to these inspection laws, only first growth leaves from each plant were sellable.[10] This policy restricted the quantity of tobacco available for export, which helped maintain higher prices for planters.[11] At an inspection, each hogshead* of tobacco leaves was opened to check for mold and evidence of poorer-quality second growth leaves. Officials burned any

---

[5] The nearest statutory school in 1706 was in Thurso, about nine miles away. James Traill Calder and Thomas Sinclair, *Sketch of the Civil and Traditional History of Caithness from the Tenth Century*, 2nd ed., (Wick, U.K.: William Roe, 1887), 221.
[6] Hancock, *Citizens of the World*, 61. For information about transatlantic tobacco trade prior to the eighteenth century, see Marcy Norton, *Sacred Gifts, Profane Pleasures: A History of Tobacco and Chocolate in the Atlantic World* (Ithaca, New York: Cornell University Press, 2008).
[7] Thomas C. Parramore, Peter C. Stewart, and Tommy L. Bogger, *Norfolk: The First Four Centuries* (Charlottesville, Virginia: University of Virginia Press, 1994), 68-69, 72, 77.
[8] Hancock, *Citizens of the World*, 62.
[9] In addition, non-inspected tobacco could not be used to repay public or private debts. See Gary M. Pecquet, "British Mercantilism and Crop Controls in the Tobacco Colonies: A Study in Rent-Seeking Costs," *Cato Journal*, 22, 3 (Winter, 2003), 467-484, ProQuest Central.
[10] Barbara Hahn, *Making Tobacco Bright: Creating an American Commodity, 1617-1937* (Baltimore, Maryland: The Johns Hopkins Press, 2011), 24.
[11] Pecquet, "British Mercantilism and Crop Controls in the Tobacco Colonies."

tobacco that did not meet the inspection standard.¹² Only once it was certified could Oswald begin haggling over the purchase price. Such practices did not fit well with Adam Smith's Enlightenment* ideas about free trade, but much of the global commerce in the eighteenth century remained rigorously controlled in accordance with mercantilist* values. Such trade was also quite profitable.¹³

In 1741, Oswald returned to Glasgow. In recognition of his work in Virginia, the Carolinas, and Jamaica, Oswald was made a partner in his cousins' firm. As a partner, Oswald aggressively advocated for an expansion of the firm's scope and mission.¹⁴ It soon entered the sugar business.

~

Sugarcane is a grass with species indigenous to both New Guinea and India. Arab traders brought the plant to the Middle East, and the Portuguese introduced it to the Madeira archipelago in the early fifteenth century. By 1452, Madeira's highly profitable sugar mill had become the primary source of Europe's sugar supply.¹⁵ Columbus carried sugarcane shoots to Hispaniola on his second voyage in 1493, where the plant found the humid environment hospitable, but it wasn't until the seventeenth century that sugarcane production exploded in the Caribbean. Barbados became the early production leader as a result of its flat topography, which was ideal for cultivation, its abundance of water and sunshine, and its being a frequent first port of call for Caribbean-bound ships.¹⁶ Initially the work force on the island consisted primarily of White¹⁷ indentured servants* and

---

[12] Hahn, *Making Tobacco Bright*, 32.
[13] Michael Kwass, "The Global Underground: Smuggling, Rebellion, and the Origins of the French Revolution," *The French Revolution in Global Perspective*, Susanne Desan, Linda Hunt and William Max Wilson (ed.) (Ithaca, New York: Cornell University Press, 2013), 15-16.
[14] Hancock, *Citizens of the World*, 62.
[15] Sidney M. Greenfield, "Madeira and the Beginnings of New World Sugar Cane Cultivation and Plantation Slavery: A Study in Institution Building," *Caribbean Slavery in the Atlantic World: A Student Reader*, Verene Shepherd and Hilary McD. Beckles (ed.) (Princeton, New Jersey: Markus Wiener Publishers, 2000), 48, 50.
[16] Ian Williams, *Rum: A Social and Sociable History* (New York: Nation Books, 2005), 19, 27-29, 48.
[17] In the wake of the protests following George Floyd's death in Minneapolis, Minnesota on May 25, 2020, the National Association of Black Journalists (NABJ) released the following statement: "it is important to capitalize 'Black' when referring to (and out of respect for) the Black diaspora. NABJ also recommends that whenever a color is used to appropriately describe race then it should be capitalized, including White and Brown." I have adopted this style recommendation as a result, except when quoting from a primary source. See National Association of Black

prisoners, but the ever-increasing demand for sugar led to the dramatic importation of African slaves, beginning in the 1650s. By 1680, there were seventeen African slaves for each White servant living in Barbados.[18]

To create the sugar sold in Thomas Dickenson's grocery store or added to the tea in the Ranelagh Gardens, African slaves began preparing the fields each July or August by burning away old cane and weeds. Then came the arduous job of sowing the tops of three sugarcane plants into a two-foot wide, three-foot long and six-to-nine-inch deep trench. This was the hardest job in the growing and production cycle and the expected work rate in the French Antilles was 28 trenches per hour. Sowing the sugarcane was done almost exclusively by the female slaves, working on what was called the Great Gang. After planting, twelve months of pruning, weeding, and irrigating followed before the cane was ready for harvest. After harvest, the cycle then began immediately again, and many plantation owners rotated their fields to allow for a nearly continuous cycle of sowing and reaping.[19]

The harvesting and processing of the sugarcane required a unique agricultural urgency.[20] It had to be prepared quickly in order to retain the maximum sugar content and to prevent natural fermentation.[21] This meant that within 48 hours the cane had to be cut at ground level, chopped into four-foot segments, transported to the mill, and crushed under the mill roll: a gear-driven machine with three great rollers that worked like a hand-cranked washing machine mangle. In the eighteenth century, a sugar mill's power came from wind, water, animals, or slaves.[22] The exigency of processing cane meant that slave women worked for eighteen to twenty hours a day pushing the cane into the rollers. If a

---

Journalists, "NABJ Statement on Capitalizing Black and Other Racial Identifiers," June 2020, accessed August 27, 2020, https://www.nabj.org/page/styleguide

[18] Hilary Mc D. Beckles and Andrew Downes, "The Economics of Transition to the Black Labour System in Barbados, 1630-1680," *Caribbean Slavery in the Atlantic World: A Student Reader*, Verene Shepherd and Hilary McD. Beckles (ed.) (Princeton, New Jersey: Markus Wiener Publishers, 2000), 240-241. "White" and "Black" are both intentionally capitalized. See Chapter F, footnote 60.

[19] Elizabeth Abbott, *Sugar: A Bittersweet History* (New York: Duckworth Overlook, 2009), 81-84, 87. The work of the Great Gang was supplemented by the work of the Second Gang, and on large plantations, the Third Gang. Slaves were assigned to the Great or Second gang based on exhaustion levels; the Third Gang consisted of children, the elderly and the disabled.

[20] Philip D. Morgan, "Slavery in the British Caribbean," *The Cambridge World History of Slavery, Volume 3: AD 1420-AD 1804*, David Eltis and Stanley L. Engerman (eds.) (New York: Cambridge University Press, 2011), 386.

[21] Williams, *Rum*, 11.

[22] Stuart M. Nisbet, "Early Glasgow Sugar Plantations in the Caribbean," *Scottish Archaeological Journal*, vol. 31, no. 1/2 (2009), 115-136, EBSCOhost.

hand got caught in the rollers, it was cut off with a machete so that nothing stopped the flow of production.[23]

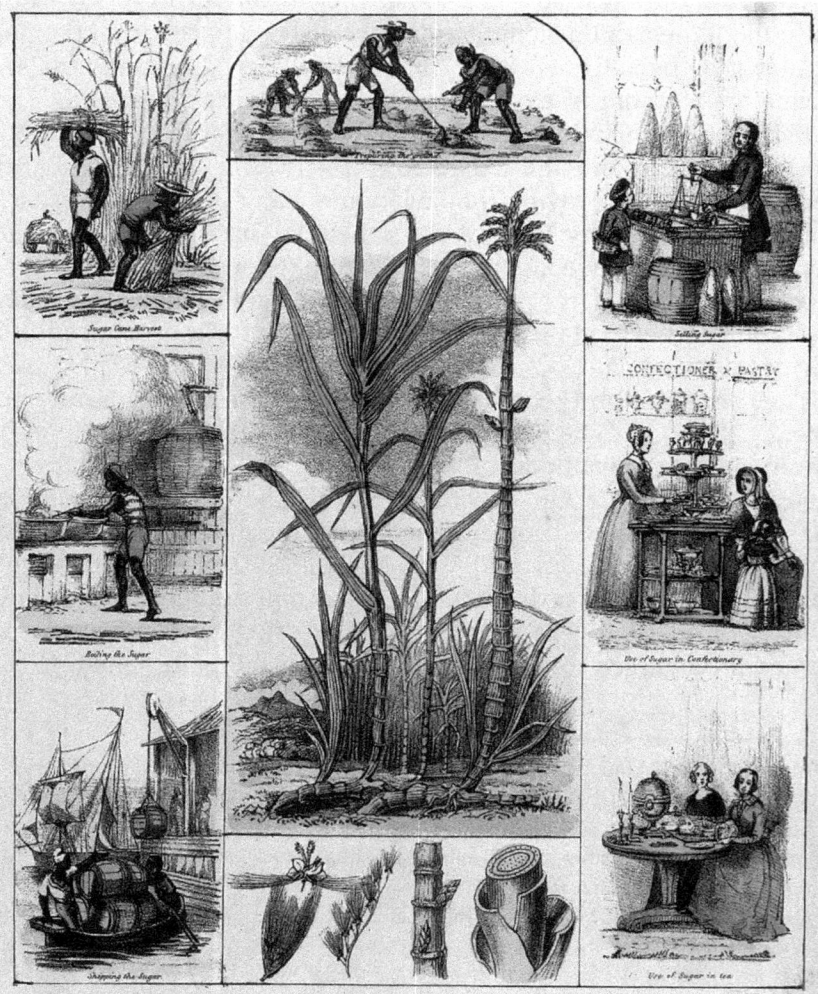

Figure 2: "A Sugar Cane Plant (Saccharum officinarum), its Flower and Sections of Stem, Bordered by Six [sic] Scenes Illustrating its Use by Man," color lithograph, c. 1840, courtesy of the Wellcome Library, London, 28057i. The surrounding scenes are labeled: preparing the ground (top); sugar cane harvest, boiling the sugar, shipping the sugar (left); and selling sugar, use of sugar in confectionery, and use of sugar in tea (right).

---

[23] Abbott, *Sugar*, 88.

The roller-crushed cane released juice, which then ran down a channel to the first boiler, where the sap was heated, quicklime was added to clarify it, and any impurities were skimmed off. The amount of quicklime needed varied tremendously, depending on the soil, fertilizer, moisture, and ripeness. The head boiler had to determine the correct amount of quicklime to add, and this determination controlled the quality of the refined sugar the crop would produce.[24] After clarification, the juice flowed to a row of additional boiling pans of decreasing size, which were progressively used to boil off more and more water to encourage crystallization. When the head boiler judged the juice in the final pan to be ready, it was ladled into earthenware vessels and allowed to set. The liquid that did not crystalize dripped out the bottom of the funnel-shaped vessel as molasses.[25] Five months after the sugarcane harvest, the earthenware held a course, brown, muscovado sugar, which was put in hogsheads and transported to Britain for further refining before wholesale and retail purchase.[26]

This production system, and the horrific human toll it exacted, brought large quantities of sugar to Britain and British consumption grew enormously in the eighteenth century as a result. In 1700, annual intake was four pounds per person, but by 1729, it had doubled to eight pounds per person. By mid-century, it was being consumed by members of all social classes and by 1789 British sugar consumption had grown to twelve pounds per person per year.[27] The demand became so great that Britain's Caribbean possessions could not produce sufficient quantities to supply the British appetite. Since the French only consumed 50% of what islands like Saint-Domingue (Haiti), Martinique, and Guadeloupe produced, much of the French Caribbean's sugar ended up being sold in Britain when the two nations were not at war.[28] The French influence also influenced the price of

---

[24] One hundred pounds of cane might need as little as two ounces or as much as three pounds of quicklime to create the desired quality. Quicklime is calcium oxide (CaO). See Abbott, *Sugar*, 91.
[25] Early Caribbean sugar producers discarded the molasses as a waste product, but when planters learned how to concentrate molasses so it would not ferment, they could sell it to New Englanders, who made it into rum. Rum became the American colonies' major export with its 143 distilleries producing 4.8 million gallons of rum per year by 1770. Rum was also used to buy slaves in Africa, debilitate Native Americans, and placate British sailors. See Williams, *Rum*, 12, 89-90, 99-102, 230-235.
[26] Nisbet, "Early Glasgow Sugar Plantations in the Caribbean."
[27] Abbott, *Sugar*, 60. This rate of consumption is small compared to the average American intake today, which is about 180 pounds a year. See Ann Louise Gittleman, "Sugar Savvy 101: The Facts about Sugar and its Kissing Cousins." *Total Health* 30, no. 1 (02, 2008): 44-45,13 ProQuest Central.
[28] Laurent Dubois, "Slavery in the French Caribbean, 1634-1804," *The Cambridge World History of Slavery, Volume 3: AD 1420-AD 1804*, David Eltis and Stanley L. Engerman (eds.) (New York: Cambridge University Press, 2011), 447.

sugar in Britain: taking advantage of their greater production and lower national consumption, French merchants undercut British prices by as much as forty percent.[29] These circumstances caused a marked drop in the retail cost of sugar throughout Britain, and made it possible for a 1774 report to state, "Sugar is so generally in use, by the existence of tea, that even the poor wretches living in almshouses will not be without it."[30] This ubiquity of sugar in the British diet changed the lives of untold millions.

~

Highly successful businessmen often benefit from a lucky break at some point in their careers. Richard Oswald's came in July 1744, when the British navy captured a French ship based in Martinique and confiscated the contents of its hold. Oswald supervised the unloading of the muscovado sugar, coffee, and cocoa in Glasgow, and placed the impounded goods in his firm's warehouse. By selling this free, unexpected merchandise and goods from other prize ships to Hamburg merchants, Oswald reportedly made £15,000. [31] The profits from his other

Figure 3: "Panorama of the River Thames and the Buildings of the City, Looking Northwards Beside London Bridge," print by S. and N. Buck, 1749, courtesy of the Wellcome Library, no. 24286i

---

[29] Andrew J. O'Shaughnessy, "The Formation of a Commercial Lobby: The West India Interest, British Colonial Policy and the American Revolution," *The Historical Journal*, Vol. 40, No. 1 (March, 1997), 71-95, EBSCOhost.
[30] Matthew Parker, *The Sugar Barons: Family, Corruption, Empire and War in the West Indies* (New York: Walker and Company, 2011), 297.
[31] The French ship was *L'Heureuse Marie*. The reason Oswald won the right to unload the French cargo rested on his partial ownership of the *Hound*, a ship commandeered by the British navy during the War of the Austrian Succession. See Hancock, *Citizens of the World*, 62. It is unclear whether or not this is the same ship and same circumstances that Hancock mentions on pages 244-245. Hancock also gives two different dates for Oswald's move to London, 1745 and mid-1746.

ventures and his own frugality made this a sufficient sum to allow Oswald to leave his cousins in Glasgow and move to London in mid-1746, where he leased a property and established his own import-export firm.

Oswald's base of operations was 17 Philpot Lane, near the heart of London's commercial and financial center in the eighteenth century.[32] The property featured a narrow, four-story brick Georgian house, which served as both an office and residence. There was also a small yard and a warehouse. The counting house's business was managed from the first floor, with the front room serving as a reception space for clients. There was also a large room for Oswald's clerks, who worked long hours and under constant scrutiny from their boss, and a small study, where Oswald held private meetings with his key financial partners. Upstairs, on the second floor, there was a dining room and a kitchen, while the

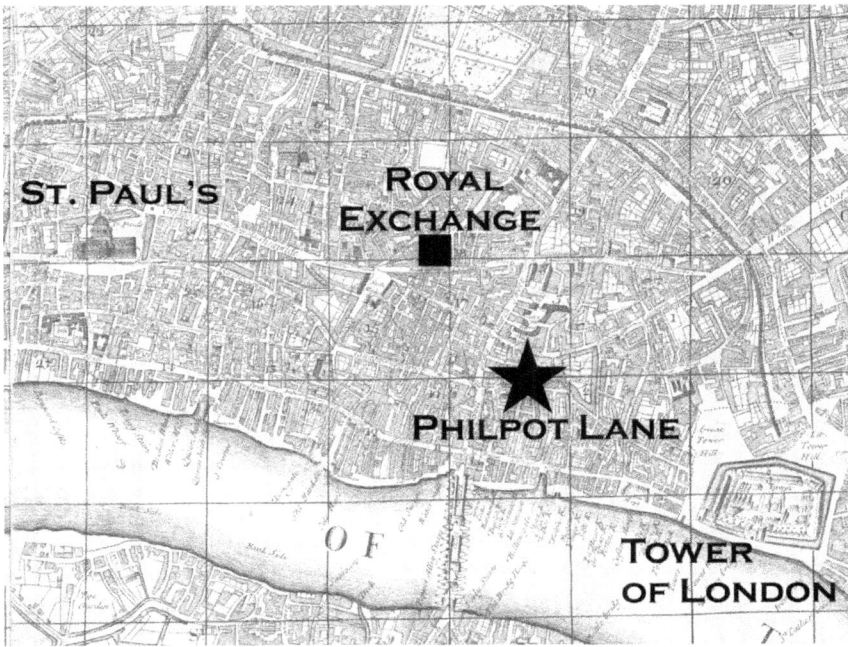

Figure 4: "A New and Exact Plan of the City's [sic] of London and Westminster, the Borough of Southwark, map by Thomas Jefferys and William Morgan, 1735" [annotated], courtesy of the Norman B. Leventhal Map & Education Center, Boston Public Library, 06_01_012246.

---

[32] Philpot Lane runs north to south; the two cross streets are Fenchurch and Eastcheap. If walking west, it is about a third of the way from the Tower of London to St. Paul's Cathedral. The nearest Tube stop is "Monument" on the Circle and District Lines.

third floor housed two bedrooms. These floors were connected by an interior staircase that ran along one side of the house. An attic provided living quarters for some of Oswald's clerks, while a basement provided storage.[33]

British billionaire Richard Branson maintains that "succeeding in business is all about making connections."[34] Oswald believed the same thing, and, upon his arrival in London, he set about trying to establish a network of contacts. He probably began at the Royal Exchange, an arcaded courtyard not far from Philpot Lane, where merchants specializing in goods from different parts of the world met with clients, beginning at noon six days a week.[35] From the Exchange, Oswald likely visited the center of all shipping news, Lloyd's Coffee House on Lombard Street. This establishment published *Lloyd's News*, which kept track of all shipping intelligence and sales. After Lloyd's, Oswald could have headed to Jonathan's Coffee House on Exchange Alley in hope of speaking with stockbrokers.[36] Despite his best efforts, Oswald did not receive a warm reception in establishments like these. This was because London's business community generally resented the Scots, both for their very presence and for their commercial success. It was extraordinarily difficult for someone from Caithness and Glasgow to penetrate London's eighteenth-century commercial networks. Oswald turned instead to formal and informal networks created by Scots who had left their homeland in search of better economic opportunities.[37] These men shared Oswald's ambition, competence, and middling socio-economic background.[38] All were in London to make their fortunes in global trade, and all understood that they needed to find inventive ways of minimizing costs. This meant eliminating as many middlemen as possible and controlling the means of production as much as possible. To achieve these goals, Oswald and his five closest associates bought their own ships, hired their own personnel, and contracted their own agents. They also decided in 1748 to purchase an island in West Africa and enter the slave trade.[39]

---

[33] Hancock, *Citizens of the World*, 91-94, 103.
[34] Richard Branson, "Richard Branson: Why You Should Network," Virgin.com, accessed January 19, 2020 http://www.virgin.com/entrepreneur/richard-branson-why-you-should-network
[35] Jerry White, *London in the 18th Century: A Great and Monstrous Thing* (London: Vintage Books, 2013), 174.
[36] Bryant Lillywhite, *London Coffee Houses: A Reference Book of Coffee Houses of the Seventeenth, Eighteenth, and Nineteenth Centuries* (London: George Allen and Unwin Ltd., 1963), 305-308, 330-335.
[37] White, *London in the 18th Century*, 94, 119-120.
[38] Hancock, *Citizens of the World*, 43-44.
[39] Oswald's closest business associates were John Augustus Boyd (1679-1765), John Boyd (1718-1800), Alexander Grant (1705-1772), John Mill (1710-1771) and John Sargent II (1714-1791).

Bance Island, a fifteen-acre islet in the middle of the Sierra Leone River, became a slave-trading center long before Grant, Oswald & Co. bought it. One owner was the English joint-stock trading monopoly, the Royal African Company (RAC). According to the terms of its September 1672 charter, the RAC possessed an exclusive right to trade in gold, silver, and slaves on the West African coast. It also had the power to build forts, raise troops, fight wars, and confiscate the property of anyone who violated its prerogatives. [40] The company experienced some financial success, but lost control of Bance Island in 1728, when the followers of a Portuguese-Senegambian slave trader attacked and destroyed the island's fortifications.[41] For the next fifteen years, the island reverted to African control and was not used for slaving. Beginning in 1744, a private citizen named George Freyer attempted to establish his own slave-trading center on Bance, but after four years of unprofitable futility he offered his rights to the island for sale. Grant, Oswald & Company purchased Bance Island on July 8, 1748[42] and set their minds to succeeding where Freyer had not.

Oswald and his partners were optimistic about their venture because they had more capital resources than Freyer did. They also knew that Bance Island's location offered several advantages over other slaving stations on the West African coast. It was situated in a broad, deep, estuarial river with protected bays, surrounded by rich timber supplies, fertile soils, abundant supplies of fish and fruit, fresh sea breezes, and ample streams with drinkable water. The island clearly benefited from its adjacent environment.[43] European visitors regularly praised Bance's setting compared to that of other destinations in the African tropics.[44] Its small size made it easier to fortify against attacks by European rivals, and its proximity to experienced slave-trading African tribes facilitated a large volume of transactions. The new proprietors did not take these advantages

---

[40] The Royal African Company (RAC) replaced previous English joint stock companies, including Royal Adventures and Gambia Adventures, operating on Bance Island and other stations on the West Coast of Africa, Bance Island is also referred to as "Bence Island" or even just as "Sierra Leone" in many sources. See K. G. Davies, *The Royal African Company* (New York: Atheneum, 1970), 30, 97-98, 388.

[41] The slave trader was José Lopes de Moura. See Hugh Thomas, *The Slave Trade: The Story of the Atlantic Slave Trade, 1440-1870* (New York: Simon & Schuster, 1997), 342, 344.

[42] David Hancock, "Scots in the Slave Trade," *Nation and Province in the First British Empire: Scotland and the Americas, 1600-1800*, Ned C. Landsman (ed.) (Lewisburg, Pennsylvania: Bucknell University Press, 2001), 67. Oswald owned a one sixth share of Grant, Oswald and Company.

[43] Hancock, *Citizens of the World*, 174.

[44] For one example of this attitude see "Report of the Commissioners Sent Out by the British Government to Investigate the State of the Settlements and Forts on the Coast of Africa." *The Monthly Magazine*, April 1, 1817, [No. 296] in *The Monthly Magazine or British Register*, Vol. XLIII, Part I for 1817 (London: Printed for Sir Richard Phillips, 1817), 203.

for granted. Instead, they took a long-term view. They invested in improvements to the island's facilities and made sure that Bance had the supplies and personnel it needed to prosper. By 1756, the walls of the island's fort had undergone significant repairs and upgrades, its defensive cannons had grown in both size and quantity, and the number of White employees had increased from ten to thirty-five. This made Bance Island one of the most secure and well-staffed White settlements in West Africa.[45]

Oswald and his colleagues also sought to reconstitute some of the fundamental assumptions of the African slave trade. The motivation for this change did not stem from moral considerations but from a desire to increase profits. For Oswald and other slave traders, Africans were simply another commodity to be traded, little different than tobacco or sugar. The questions that kept them up at night were not concerned with the ethics of brutally uprooting millions of humans and transporting them to a foreign land to suffer a life of bondage. Rather, what concerned Oswald and his kin were simply the pertinent economic considerations. Consequently, the partners insisted upon upholding two protocols they believed would produce greater profits.

First and foremost, Grant, Oswald & Company sought to maintain peaceful and positive relationships with local African kings. Bance Island managers, known as agents, were expressly forbidden from kidnapping slaves or waging war on local tribes.[46] This was because the company relied upon these local tribes to provide them with the slaves needed in the Americas. The company fostered positive relationships with these tribes by honoring the prices set by African chiefs. On Bance, transactions were made one slave at a time through a system of bartering. In exchange for each slave, agents offered guns, gunpowder, alcohol, beads, toys, knives, crystal, and seventeen different fabrics, ranging from Indian cottons and Persian silks to German linens and Scottish tartans. In return, the company purchased no fewer than 12,929 individuals between 1748 and 1784, most of whom came from non-coastal areas. The specifics as to how these people were acquired by the coastal tribes in Sierra Leone remains unclear, but war and demographic and economic changes contributed substantially.[47] What is certain is that the region did not have institutionalized slavery prior to development of the Atlantic slave trade and that coastal African chiefs came to control access to slaves in Sierra Leone once that trade began in earnest. This differs from other parts of West Africa, where slavery existed prior to the arrival of the Europeans and where both Christian and Muslim slave traders ventured into the interior

---

[45] Hancock, *Citizens of the World*, 188.
[46] Hancock, *Citizens of the World*, 199.
[47] Hancock, "Scots in the Slave Trade," 74-75; and Hancock, *Citizens of the World*, 213, 218.

themselves.⁴⁸ By the eighteenth century, most West Africans who became slaves were prisoners of war, convicted criminals, debtors, sold by relatives, or kidnapped by other Africans.⁴⁹

Second, Grant, Oswald & Company changed the method by which most slave ships acquired their cargos. Along much of the West African coast, ship captains typically conducted their business on board, waiting offshore as their holds slowly filled. This could take as long as five months. The longer the loading took, the more likely the loss of lives.⁵⁰ On Bance Island, however, the trade was conducted at the fort, and the company's agents always tried to have slaves to sell so the ship captains could fill their holds quickly. Not waiting offshore saved lives, improved profit margins, and meant that Bance Island slaves were sold to ship captains at premium prices.⁵¹

Once Oswald and his associates had Bance Island upgraded and fully operational, the horrid commerce began in earnest. Some of Oswald's ships participated in the traditional triangular trade route, running from Britain to Africa to the Americas and back to Britain. One such early voyage was of the seventy-ton sloop *Carlisle*, captained by Thomas Osborne. It left London on February 1, 1756, loaded with goods from Europe and Asia for African kings, and it arrived off the Senegambia coast six weeks later. Osborne purchased 35 slaves in the region and then proceeded to Bance Island, where he unloaded most of his cargo and replaced it with 158 slaves who had been held in the island's slave yard. Osborne set sail for what was then known as Charles Town, South Carolina with a total of 193 slaves, chained into place in the hull's claustrophobic half decks, lying down shoulder to shoulder. The Atlantic crossing, or Middle Passage, of the ship's triangular trade journey must have been particularly gruesome: the *Carlisle* arrived in Charleston on June 28 with only 150 slaves,⁵² a mortality rate of 22%. The conditions on the ship must have been at least as grim as those described by former slave Olaudah Equiano, who endured the Atlantic crossing in 1756:

---

⁴⁸ G. Ugo Nwokeji, "Slavery in Non-Islamic West Africa, 1420-1820," *The Cambridge World History of Slavery, Volume 3: AD 1420-AD 1804*, David Eltis and Stanley L. Engerman (eds.) (New York: Cambridge University Press, 2011), 86, 91.
⁴⁹ Thomas, *The Slave Trade*, 372-273.
⁵⁰ Thomas, *The Slave Trade*, 406.
⁵¹ Hancock, *Citizens of the World*, 199.
⁵² "Voyage 75237, *Carlisle* (1756)," *Voyages: The Trans-Atlantic Slave Trade Database*, accessed January 17, 2020, http://www.slavevoyages.org/voyage/75237/variables. The death rate for slaves on all British ships fell from 10% to 5.65% over the course of the eighteenth century. See Thomas, *The Slave Trade*, 423. The calculated mortality rate on British ships for the whole of the slave trade was about 13%. See Morgan, "Slavery in the British Caribbean," 382.

> The stench of the hold while we were on the coast was so intolerably loathsome, that it was dangerous to remain there for anytime... but now that the whole ship's cargo were confined together, it became absolutely pestilential. The closeness of the place, and the heat of the climate, added to the number in the ship, which was so crowded that each had scarcely room to turn himself, almost suffocated us. This is produced copious perspirations, so that the air soon became unfit for respiration, from a variety of loathsome smells, and brought on a sickness among the slaves, of which many died.[53]

Those who did survive the Middle Passage were traumatized in other ways, for in addition to humiliation, rape, and torture, there was the disorientation and psychological shock of being uprooted from everything they had ever known. As one ship surgeon noted in 1790,

> The slaves in the night were often heard making a howling melancholy kind of noise, something expressive of extreme anguish. I repeatedly ordered the woman, who had been my interpreter in the later part of the voyage, to inquire into the particular causes of this very melancholy noise. She answered that it was because the slaves had dreamed they were back in their own country, only to wake to the reality of the slave ship.[54]

Once the *Carlisle* arrived in Charleston, the Africans were sold on Oswald's behalf. There were also nine "privileged" slaves, which meant that Captain Osborne sold them on his own for his personal profit.[55] All of the *Carlisle* slaves

---

[53] Olaudah Equiano, *The Life of Olaudah Equiano: or Gustavus Vassa, the African* (Boston, Massachusetts: Isaac Knapp, 1837), 47. Equiano was born in 1745 in a place he called Essaka in the Kingdom of Benin. He purchased his freedom in 1766, became a leading abolitionist in London, and published his vivid memoir in 1789.

[54] Thomas Trotter quoted in Dorothy Schneider and Carl J. Schneider, *An Eyewitness History of Slavery in America: From Colonial Times to the Civil War* (New York: Checkmark Books/Facts on File, 2000), 46.

[55] A letter from Henry Laurens to Richard Oswald says that the *Carlisle* only shipped 141 slaves, including 120 from Bance Island. Laurens also states that only five were lost crossing the Atlantic and that all but three were in good health upon arrival. If Laurens' numbers are correct, instead of those used in the Slavevoyages.org database, then the mortality rate abroad the *Carlisle* was only 3.34%. Both sources agree that nine slaves were designated as "privileged." See Henry Laurens to Richard Oswald, June 29, 1756 in *The Papers of Henry Laurens*, Volume 2, November 1, 1755-December 31, 1758, Philip M Hamer and George C. Rogers, Jr. (eds.) (Columbia, South Carolina: University of South Carolina Press, 1970), 233.

who disembarked in South Carolina then risked joining the vast numbers who died within three years of their arrival in the Americas.56

The *Carlisle* landed in Charleston instead of in Barbados or Jamaica because by January 1756 Oswald had established a special commercial relationship with a local businessman, Henry Laurens. Oswald trusted Laurens and offered him exclusive rights to sell Bance Island slaves in Charleston. Evidence for this trust can be seen in the earliest surviving letter between the two men. Dated April 13, 1756, it was Laurens' response to Oswald's letter of January 17. Laurens tells Oswald that as a result of the falling prices for slaves in Charleston, "we sincerely wish you may order the Sloop [*Carlisle*] to a much better market than ours at present seems to promise."57 It was also Laurens' practice to

Figure 5: 1) "Henry Laurens Esqr.," print by Valentine Green after John Singleton Copley, 1782, courtesy of Yale University Art Gallery, 1946.9.935;

---

56 The percentage of slaves who died within three years of arrival in the British Caribbean fell over the course of the eighteenth century from approximately one third of the slaves at mid-century to a quarter in 1790. Clearly, the physical and psychological adjustment to the New World remained extraordinarily difficult for a large percentage of those taken from Africa. In the Thirteen Colonies, the slave population sustained itself through natural procreation, but it is unlikely that those who emerged from the Middle Passage greatly enfeebled would live beyond three years. See Philip D. Morgan, "Slavery in the British Caribbean," *The Cambridge World History of Slavery, Volume 3: AD 1420-AD 1804*, David Eltis and Stanley L. Engerman (eds.) (New York: Cambridge University Press, 2011), 382 and Richard Hofstadter, *America at 1750: A Social Portrait* (New York: Vintage Books, 1973), 90-92, 112-113.
57 Henry Laurens to Richard Oswald, April 13, 1756 in *The Papers of Henry Laurens*, Volume 2, 169. Given the time it took for letters to cross the Atlantic, Oswald could not redirect the *Carlisle* to another port of call, but in this case the symbolism was more important than the practicality.

share all the financial risks with his slaving partners.⁵⁸ Oswald deeply valued such honesty and financial integrity, which was why he was willing to pay Laurens a 9% commission on the sale of each slave sent from Bance Island to Charleston.⁵⁹ Laurens also saw to the outfitting of the *Carlisle* for the last leg of the archetypal triangle route, loading the ship's hold with South Carolinian rice. Captain Osborne and his small crew returned to London on December 29, 1756 after a 195-day journey.⁶⁰

Oswald-owned and Company-owned ships did not always participate in traditional triangular trade. Like many other ships plying the Atlantic, Oswald's vessels also took other routes. On August 5, 1760, for example, the one hundred and fifty-ton *Bance Island* set sail from Charleston, bound for Sierra Leone. The ship loaded 352 slaves in Africa and returned to South Carolina on May 30, 1761. Records indicate that 300 slaves survived the trip, giving the voyage a 14.77% mortality rate.⁶¹ Similarly, a decade later, the one hundred-and-eighty-two ton *Charlotte* made the same out-and-back journey. When this ship returned to Charleston on September 5, 1771, the captain reported that only 118 of the 139 slaves leaving Bance Island had survived, giving the trip a mortality rate of 15.11%.⁶² Not all of Oswald's ships suffered such high

Figure 6: "To be sold, on board the ship Bance Island, ... negroes, just arrived from the Windward & Rice Coast," advertisement, unknown date, courtesy of the Schomburg Center for Research in Black Culture, The New York Public Library, b16104370.

---

⁵⁸ James Rawley, *London, Metropolis of the Slave Trade* (Columbia, Missouri: University Press, 2003), 89, EBSCOebooks.
⁵⁹ Henry Laurens to Richard Oswald, May 24, 1768 in *The Papers of Henry Laurens*, Volume 5, September 1, 1765-July 31, 1768, George C. Rogers, Jr. and David R. Chesnutt (eds.) (Columbia, South Carolina: University of South Carolina Press, 1976), 694. In an effort to reassure Oswald that he is getting a good deal, Laurens notes in this same letter that other Charleston merchants charge a 13% commission and "sometimes more."
⁶⁰ Rawley, *London, Metropolis of the Slave Trade*, 92.
⁶¹ "Voyage 26022, *Bance Island* (1760)," *Voyages: The Trans-Atlantic Slave Trade Database*, accessed January 19, 2020, http://www.slavevoyages.org/voyage/26022/variables
⁶² "Voyage 78278, *Charlotte* (1771)," *Voyages: The Trans-Atlantic Slave Trade Database*, accessed January 19, 2020, http://www.slavevoyages.org/voyage/78278/variables

losses or went to and from Charleston. In 1786, the one hundred-and-ten-ton *Mary* loaded 154 slaves at Bance Island and gained two more during the Middle Passage with the birth of two babies. The ship arrived in St. Kitts with 156 men, women, and children and eventually disembarked 151, a mortality rate of 1.95%.[63] Overall, the thirty-three voyages completed by Oswald-owned or partially-owned ships between 1752 and 1787 had a 13.41% fatality rate.[64] This was higher than the overall British average, but even with these loses, as well as the expenses of shipping, insurance, piracy, wages, and overhead, Oswald still made money as a slaver. These profits, between 6% and 10%, were not dramatically different, however, from those of other slavers or from merchants not trading in people.[65] It was not necessary for a mid-eighteenth-century merchant to engage in human trafficking to make a profit. This makes the moral status of those who did more troubling and their financial rationale more dubious.

~

In summer 1758, Oswald won a bid to supply bread to the British army fighting in the Seven Years' War in Germany.[66] On the European continent, this war stemmed as much from a diplomatic upheaval as it did from the British-French colonial rivalry that Monckton witnessed. Oswald was less concerned with the details of Austria's *rapprochement* with France in the wake of Prussia's rise than he was with the arrival of a lucrative new business opportunity.[67] He won the bread contract both by luck and by strategy. On the lucky side, none of the

---

[63] "Voyage 82604, *Mary* (1786)," *Voyages: The Trans-Atlantic Slave Trade Database*, accessed January 19, 2020, http://www.slavevoyages.org/voyage/82604/variables

[64] I have computed this percentage based on the records available in the slavevoyages.org database. This percentage is too high if Henry Lauren's numbers for the *Carlisle*'s 1756 trip, as discussed in footnote 54, are correct.

[65] Thomas, *The Slave Trade*, 444. Countries began to abolish their participation in the slave trade as it became unprofitable. The Danes, for example, abolished their slave trade in 1792 specifically for this reason. See James A. Rawley, *The Transatlantic Slave Trade: A History* (New York: W. W. Norton & Company, 1981), 265, 267.

[66] This war is known as the French and Indian War (1754-1763) in American history.

[67] Isser Woloch, *Eighteenth-Century Europe: Tradition and Progress, 1715-1789* (New York: W. W. Norton & Company, 1982), 41. Prussia's rise under Frederick William I and Frederick the Great threatened Austria's domination of central Europe. After the Prussians captured Silesia during the War of the Austrian Succession (1740-1748), the Habsburgs looked to their traditional enemy, France, to balance Prussia's gains. This produced a diplomatic realignment with Britain, Prussia and Russia pitted against France and Austria.

conventional provisioners submitted bids, forcing the army to ask for bids from the public. On the strategic side, Oswald's bid was quite low: he agreed to provide bread for the first year of the contract for 75% of the pre-war market rate, undercutting the only other offer. Once he had the contract, Oswald looked to control the means of production as much as possible. He moved to Germany with his wife, Mary Ramsay, who was the only heir of a wealthy Jamaican plantation owner. Upon his arrival in Germany, Oswald set up his own supply depots and bakeries, hired his own employees, and built a few mills to grind the wheat into flour. His reliable deliveries of millions of loaves encouraged the army to renew his contract, but when it did so Oswald charged the army 8% more than the market rate. His third contract had a mark-up of 143%, which is why he made a £112,000 fortune on bread by the end of the war.[68] Little wonder Scottish poet Robert Burns referred to Oswald in a bitter ode as the "Plunderer of Armies!"[69]

In September 1761, a newly-appointed First Commissary-General, Thomas Pownall, conducted a tour of British supply depots and magazines in Germany to ferret out embezzlement, negligence, falsification of records, and shoddy goods.[70] One night, after inspecting Oswald's bread depot in Kassel and finding everything in in good shape, Pownall and Oswald shared an evening meal together. As the former colonial governor of Massachusetts and the former Virginia merchant traded stories about their years in the American colonies, the combination of tales and wine ignited Oswald's desire to own land in the Thirteen Colonies or Canada.[71] An uncharacteristic nostalgia also seems to have influenced Oswald, now in his mid-fifties and thirty years removed from his life in Virginia. The enticing possibilities from Nova Scotia to Florida cried out to Oswald like a siren.

Oswald chose to invest in land in newly-acquired Florida.[72] In July 1764, he won the right to survey 20,000 acres on the east Florida coast. True to form, he was one of the first men to win this right. Oswald had to then find someone to select the particular area, survey it, and register that survey with the provisional governor. Once the survey was registered, the governor awarded the land grant with the provision that the land be settled with White Protestants within a

---

[68] Hancock, *Citizens of the World*, 221, 227, 231, 233-234, 236-237. Specifically, Oswald delivered 5,395,426 loaves of bread during the war, for which the army paid £191,088. Oswald's costs were just £79,000, leaving him with a handsome profit.

[69] Robert Burns, "Ode, Sacred To The Memory Of Mrs. Oswald Of Auchencruive," *Burns Country*, accessed December 3, 2015, http://www.robertburns.org/works/245.shtml

[70] Charles Assheton Whately Pownall, *Thomas Pownall, M. P., F. R. S., Governor of Massachusetts Bay, Author of the Letters of Junius* (London: Henry Stevens, Son & Stiles, 1908), 167-168.

[71] Hancock, *Citizens of the World*, 153.

[72] Britain acquired East Florida (the non-panhandle part of the modern state) from Spain in the Treaty of Paris (1763), which ended the Seven Years' War.

decade.[73] Oswald naturally turned to Henry Laurens to find someone to complete these tasks for him. The surveyor Laurens selected a plot of land forty-five miles south of St. Augustine and ten miles north of modern Daytona Beach at the confluence of the Halifax River and Tomoka River and with access to the sea via the Ponce de Leon Inlet. From the outset, however, Laurens was not enthusiastic about the undertaking. He wrote to Oswald:

> Your views of establishing a Farm, plantation & Vineyard in our back settlements, are commendable, Generous & the principles upon which they are extended truly noble; nevertheless, I must not flatter but plainly tell you that the carrying of them into effect, tho not impracticable, will be attended with more difficulty & more expense of Money than you seem to apprehend....The first difficulty that you will encounter is that of obtaining a Sufficient quantity of good land in one body.[74]

Laurens issued a similar warning a few months later, but by February 1765 he had taken out advertisements seeking slaves to work on Oswald's East Florida plantation:

> WANTED, Two Negro Carpenters, two Coopers, three pair of Sawyers, forty Field Negroes, young men and women, some acquainted with indico [sic] making, and all with the ordinary course of Planation work in this country; for which good prices will be given, in cash, or bills upon London: And in cases of no bargain, secrecy if required, may be depended on. — Any person having such Negroes to sell please apply to
> HENRY LAURENS[75]

Despite his misgivings, Laurens purchased the slaves and hired an overseer. The slaves cleared 400 acres, planted indigo and sugar cane, erected barns and stables, and built modest housing to forge the Mount Oswald settlement out of the swamp. By 1770, a sugar mill, distillery, and warehouse had been constructed, and Oswald supplemented the work force with additional slaves

---

[73] George C. Rogers Jr., "The East Florida Society of London, 1766-1767," *The Florida Historical Quarterly*, vol. 54, no. 4 (April, 1976), 479-496, EBSCOhost.
[74] Henry Laurens to Richard Oswald, July 7, 1764 in *The Papers of Henry Laurens*, Volume 4, September 1, 1763-August 31, 1765, George C. Rogers, Jr. and David R. Chesnutt (eds.) (Columbia, South Carolina: University of South Carolina Press, 1974), 332-333.
[75] "Advertisement, *The Gazette*, February 23, 1765," in *The Papers of Henry Laurens*, Volume 4, 584.

from Africa.[76] In 1767, 106 Africans arrived from Bance Island.[77] They were followed by the arrival of the *Charlotte* in 1771 with 115 slaves, and the *Betsy* in 1774 with 82 slaves.[78] By 1780, there were 230 slaves working on Oswald's Florida plantation.[79] These men and women faced unspeakable violence and brutality. In fact, the conditions were such that Oswald's slaves murdered their overseer during a slave rebellion in 1767.[80] Others sought escape, and, like slaves from other nearby plantations, may have joined maroon communities, allied themselves with the Seminoles, joined Black militias organized by the British to protect Florida during the American Revolution, or sought refuge in Spanish Florida after

Figure 7: Marker in Tomoka State Park by the Volusia County Historical Commission, commemorating the existence of the Mt. Oswald Plantation. Derek Dwight Anderson photograph, July 2016.

---

[76] Hancock, *Citizens of the World*, 159.

[77] Jane Landers, *Black Society in Spanish Florida* (Urbana, Illinois: University of Illinois Press, 1999), 158.

[78] The *Charlotte* had a mortality rate of 10.16%. See "Voyage 75267, *Charlotte* (1770)," *Voyages: The Trans-Atlantic Slave Trade Database*, accessed January 19, 2020, http://slavevoyages.org/voyage/75267/variables. The jointly-owned *Betsy* departed from another slave island, Iles de Los, off the coast from Conakry, Guinea and landed in St. Augustine with a mortality rate of 9.9%. See, "Voyage 78157, *Betsey* (1774)," *Voyages: The Trans-Atlantic Slave Trade Database*, accessed January 19, 2020, http://www.slavevoyages.org/voyage/78157/variables.

[79] Hancock, *Citizens of the World*, 162.

[80] Lucy B. Wayne, *Sweet Cane: The Architecture of the Sugar Works of East Florida* (Tuscaloosa: University Alabama Press, 2010), 54, EBSCOebooks. The name of this overseer was Samuel Huey or Samuel Hewie. It is unclear how control over the plantation was reestablished, but his replacement was a Native American or mixed-race man named Johnson, who stayed for less than a year. Subsequently, Lt. John Fairlamb, Donald McLean, and Frederick Robinson were in charge of the plantation.

1784.[81] Still others were recaptured or died attempting to free themselves from bondage.

Oswald would not be the last person in Florida's history to lose money pursuing an ill-conceived dream.[82] In Oswald's case, the causes of his problems were numerous. His plantation had poor drainage so the land could not produce sugar cane or indigo of sufficient quality to compete in the marketplace. In fact, the land was poorly suited for growing anything but rice, but rice was a crop in which Oswald had little interest; he could never reconcile his agricultural biases with the location's realities. Unlike Bance Island, Mount Oswald lacked easy access to a viable harbor, which made getting supplies to the plantation difficult, and he never found an overseer he could trust.[83] All of this meant that Oswald never saw any favorable return from his Florida investments. As Laurens succinctly said, Oswald's land would "never make any great progress…for want of Neighbours, Navigation & Markets."[84] Truthfully, this shouldn't have surprised the normally sensible Scot. He had been forewarned well before specious, rosy accounts of Florida's climate and topography reached London, but Oswald ignored Laurens' advice and instead helped fuel the speculation in Florida.[85] The misadventure in Florida was the only poor business decision of Oswald's life, but by this point his financial position was such that he could afford such a mistake.

---

[81] See Larry E. Rivers, *Slavery in Florida: Territorial Days to Emancipation* (Gainesville: University Press of Florida, 2000), 6, EBSCOebooks; Sylviane A. Diouf, *Slavery's Exiles: The Story of the American Maroons* (New York: New York University Press, 2014), 40, 44-47, 49-50, 54-56; and Edward Mair, "Slaves and Indians," *History Today* 10, 2 (February 2020), 58–69, EBSCOhost.

[82] See, for example, Edward E. Baptist, *Creating an Old South: Middle Florida's Plantation Frontier Before the Civil War* (Chapel Hill, University of North Carolina Press, 2002), 37-47; Gregg M. Turner, *The Florida Land Boom of the 1920s* (Jefferson, North Carolina: McFarland & Company, 2015), 3-5; and Trevor Burnard, *Planters, Merchants, and Slaves: Plantation Societies in British America, 1650-1820* (Chicago, Illinois: University of Chicago Press, 2015), 128-129.

[83] Hancock, *Citizens of the World*, 160, 162, 165-167. The overseer was the person who was "ultimately responsible for a profitable return on his employer's investment." See Tristan Stubbs, *Masters of Violence: The Plantation Overseers of Eighteenth-Century Virginia, South Carolina, and Georgia* (Columbia, South Carolina: University of South Carolina Press, 2018), 1, EBSCOebooks. Stubbs argues that because of this economic relationship, the "implacably violent, sadistically capricious overseer was largely atypical." (3) He also notes the difficulties Oswald and Laurens had in securing an overseer (40, 42).

[84] Henry Laurens to Richard Oswald, August 12, 1766 in *The Papers of Henry Laurens*, Volume 5, 156.

[85] Early accounts of Florida visitors dramatically shaped impressions in London; these included accounts by William Stork (1766), botanist John Bartram (1766), and Andrew Turnbull (1767). None of these accounts were accurate. See Rogers Jr., "The East Florida Society of London, 1766-1767."

~

On August 13, 1780, during the American War of Independence, Henry Laurens departed Philadelphia with orders from the Continental Congress to sail to Holland aboard the brigantine *Mercury*. His mission was to "endeavor to borrow Money any where in Europe on Account of the United States of America."[86] Twenty-two days into the voyage, Lauren's ship was overtaken and captured by the twenty-eight gun British frigate *Vestal*, captained by George Keppel. As the *Vestal* approached, Laurens ordered his most important papers to be burned or thrown overboard. A few minutes later, he ordered his remaining papers destroyed as well, but these did not immediately sink and Keppel's crew fished them out of the ocean and dried them out. Keppel determined that none of the recovered documents contained Laurens' mail and said, "you must certainly have destroyed your Mail, [for] I find nothing of any [subs]tance among these Papers."[87] Laurens admitted that this was correct, and Keppel took Laurens into custody. The *Vestal* then sailed for St. John's, Newfoundland, where Rear Admiral Richard Edwards received Laurens as a gentleman, even after Laurens offered a toast to George Washington instead of King George III. By then end of September, Laurens landed as a prisoner in England and though quite ill was "Committed to the Tower of London on 'suspicion of high Treason'" on October 6.[88] According to the judgment, Laurens was to be guarded around the clock, could not receive letters or visitors, could not have any writing materials, and was not permitted to converse. Locked in two small rooms, together "about 20 feet square," Laurens had to provide for his own food, bedding, and candles for the duration of his internment, as was true of other prisoners of the era.[89] Fortunately, Laurens did not face the absolute confinement prescribed by the court. His slave George was admitted to the Tower October 6, he received his first note from London

---

[86] Henry Laurens, "Journal and Narrative of Capture and Confinement in the Tower of London, August 13, 1780-April 4, 1782," in *The Papers of Henry Laurens*, Volume 15, December 11, 1778-August 31, 1782, David R. Chesnutt and C. James Taylor (eds.) (Columbia, South Carolina: University of South Carolina Press, 2000), 332.

[87] Laurens, "Journal and Narrative of Capture and Confinement in the Tower of London" 334.

[88] Laurens, "Journal and Narrative of Capture and Confinement in the Tower of London," 336, 338, 341.

[89] Laurens, "Journal and Narrative of Capture and Confinement in the Tower of London," 341, 343-344.

businessman William Manning on October 8, and Laurens' son, Harry, joined Manning as the prisoner's first visitors on October 14.[90]

Laurens' most important advocate throughout his fifteen-month imprisonment in Tower of London was Oswald. The two men were no longer merely business associates as in the 1750s. Rather, they were close friends. Their friendship began in the early 1770s when Laurens came to England with his three sons to visit the Low Countries, France, and Switzerland and to place his sons in schools in Geneva and England. A typical letter to Oswald from this period finds Laurens casually and conversationally sharing news about his sons, the weather, affairs in France, and his inability to meet Voltaire because of the *philosophe*'s fading health.[91] Similarly, when Laurens prepared to return to South Carolina in September 1774, he wrote to Oswald a letter that expressed a debt of friendship, rather than merely a debt of hospitality.[92] While the American Revolution certainly created tensions between the men, as well as a three-year break in their correspondence, their enduring friendship drove Oswald to look for a solution to Laurens' predicament.[93] The two men met in the Tower for the first time on January 3, 1781, after Oswald returned from a long visit to Scotland. Immediately after that visit, Oswald wrote government officials advocating for Laurens' release on parole.[94] Oswald "pledged the whole of his fortune" as collateral for Laurens' good conduct upon release. He served as a liaison between Laurens and the British government, kept Laurens informed about public opinion, submitted lengthy accounts of Laurens' assessment of the political situation in the Colonies, and provided Laurens with food and money.[95] Though these awkward months, Oswald consistently had to walk the line between remaining a loyal British subject and being a friend to the proud American.

---

[90] Laurens, "Journal and Narrative of Capture and Confinement in the Tower of London," 344-345.

[91] Henry Laurens to Richard Oswald, May 31, 1773 in *The Papers of Henry Laurens*, Volume 9, April 19, 1773-December 12, 1774, George C. Rogers, Jr. and David R. Chesnutt (eds.) (Columbia, South Carolina: University of South Carolina Press, 1981), 55-57.

[92] Henry Laurens to Richard Oswald, September 22, 1774 in *The Papers of Henry Laurens*, Volume 9, 571-574.

[93] Laurens wrote to Oswald January 4, 1775, but Oswald did not acknowledge that letter until April 12, 1778. Oswald describes the lapse as a "long & unpleasant interval." See Richard Oswald to Henry Laurens, April 12, 1778 in *The Papers of Henry Laurens*, Volume 8, March 16, 1778-July 6, 1778, David R. Chesnutt and C. James Taylor (eds.) (Columbia, South Carolina: University of South Carolina Press, 1992), 107.

[94] Richard Oswald, "Note by Richard Oswald," January 3, 1781 in *The Papers of Henry Laurens*, Volume 15, December 11, 1778-August 31, 1782, David R. Chesnutt and C. James Taylor (eds.) (Columbia, South Carolina: University of South Carolina Press, 2000), 351.

[95] Laurens, "Journal and Narrative of Capture and Confinement in the Tower of London," 355, 358-359, 364, 374, 379, 381.

Laurens' release came partially from the work of Edmund Burke. In the aftermath of the American victory at Yorktown, Burke criticized the prisoner exchange system in Parliament and used Laurens as a prime example of the problems he believed existed. This led to a decision to release Laurens on bail while awaiting trial.[96] On December 31, 1781, Laurens left the Tower in a sedan chair, too weak to walk, and appeared before the court, which set bail at £8,000. Oswald posted £2,000, Oswald's nephew, Alexander Anderson, posted another £2,000, and Laurens posted the balance.[97] Three days later, Laurens left for Bath in hope that its famed waters would prove restorative.

~

On April 7, 1782, Oswald and Laurens departed London to cross the English Channel, seemingly as friends on a vacation. Once the two men landed at Ostend, however, they headed in opposite directions. Oswald traveled south on a secret diplomatic mission to meet with Benjamin Franklin in Paris, while Laurens proceeded north to meet with John Adams, who was trying to secure diplomatic recognition and loans in the Dutch Republic.[98] Oswald's mission was to begin sounding out Franklin about possible peace terms as a result of the growing opposition in Britain to the war with its American colonies.[99] Oswald's selection for this errand was odd in many ways. He was seventy-seven years old, had no diplomatic experience, had never been to France, and by his own assessment could not speak French properly.[100] He was also blind in one eye and used an ear horn to help him hear.[101] Despite these limitations, the Secretary of State for Home, Colonial, and Irish Affairs, Lord Shelburne, specifically chose Oswald for

---

[96] David Duncan Wallace, *The Life of Henry Laurens*, (New York: G. P. Putnam's Sons, 1915), 388-389.
[97] Laurens, "Journal and Narrative of Capture and Confinement in the Tower of London," 396-397.
[98] Laurens, "Journal and Narrative of Capture and Confinement in the Tower of London," 401-402.
[99] A House of Commons resolution in February 1782 condemned the war, while one in March essentially called for the recognition of American independence. See David Schoenbrun, *Triumph in Paris: The Exploits of Benjamin Franklin* (New York: Harper & Row Publishers, 1976), 351, 353.
[100] Richard Oswald, "Richard Oswald's Journal, April 18, 1782," *The Emerging Nation: A Documentary History of the Foreign Relations of the United States Under the Articles of Confederation, 1780-1789*, Mary A. Giunta (ed.) (Washington, DC: National Historical Publications and Records Commission, 1996), 348-349.
[101] David McCullough, *John Adams* (New York: Simon & Schuster, 2001), 278 and Hancock, *Citizens of the World*, 65.

the mission in hope of appealing to Franklin. Oswald and Franklin were born within a year of one another, were both Physiocrats* and admirers of Adam Smith, and had met at least once, at a London meeting of the East Florida Society in 1765.[102] Oswald was also respected for his expertise with regard to the American colonies, and British officials consulted with him regularly during the war. As early as February 1775, for example, Oswald had submitted his plan for separating one of the southern colonies from the rest of the rebellious states to take advantage of regional differences; his advice was to try to force a divide between the southern aristocracy and what he called the "Mob of Northern Yeomen," who represented little more than a "Confederacy of Smugglers."[103] More significantly, in August 1781, Oswald had written a memorandum criticizing General Charles Cornwallis' decision to move his troops from the Carolinas to Virginia. He had specifically noted that the Chesapeake Bay would have to be secured by the British navy to prevent an entrapment of Cornwallis' troops.[104] Proved correct by the results of the Battle of Yorktown, Oswald's views held cachet. It also helped that Oswald was, in the words of a contemporary, "devoid of the pride of aristocracy without being suspected of democracy," and that King George III thought Oswald to be the "fittest Instrument for the renewal of...friendly intercourse" between the British and the Americans.[105]

A week after departing London, Oswald arrived in Paris, having experienced several frustrating, if rather typical, eighteenth century travel delays. On the morning of April 15, he went to Franklin's residence in Passy and presented his letters of introduction.[106] As the two men conversed, Oswald made it clear that he was there as a private individual, not as an official representative of the British government. He suggested that it might be desirable for both the British and the Americans to negotiate a separate peace from that with the French.[107] Franklin said that the Americans could only act in concert with France, and suggested that the British should offer the Americans all of Canada as a sign of good faith. Oswald hid his surprise about Franklin's opening offer well, and asked to take Franklin's

---

[102] Hancock, *Citizens of the World*, 391 and Schoenbrun, *Triumph in Paris*, 355.
[103] Richard Oswald quoted in W. Stitt Robinson, Jr., "Richard Oswald: Advisor to the British Ministry on the Conduct of the American Revolution," *Richard Oswald's Memorandum: On the Folly of Invading Virginia, the Strategic Importance of Portsmouth, and the Need for Civilian Control of the Military*, W. Stitt Robinson, Jr. (ed.) (Charlottesville, Virginia: University of Virginia Press, 1953), 44-45.
[104] Richard Oswald, "Memorandum 15 Augt" in *Richard Oswald's Memorandum: On the Folly of Invading Virginia, the Strategic Importance of Portsmouth, and the Need for Civilian Control of the Military*, W. Stitt Robinson, Jr. (ed.) (Charlottesville, Virginia: University of Virginia Press, 1953), 12-14, 20.
[105] Benjamin Vaughan and George III quoted in Hancock, *Citizens of the World*, 390-391.
[106] In 1782, Passy was just outside of Paris. Today, Passy is in the 16th Arrondissement.
[107] Oswald, "Richard Oswald's Journal, April 18, 1782," 345-346.

written comments back to London to consult with Shelburne.[108] Franklin agreed, but first wanted Oswald to go with him to Versailles to meet the French foreign minister, Charles Gravier, Comte de Vergennes. Franklin and Oswald did so on April 18. Vergennes kept the two guests waiting a half hour, paid Oswald a series of condescending compliments upon their introduction, and then asked him if he could speak any French. Vergennes' secretary replied that Oswald understood French, but only if His Excellency spoke slowly.[109] Vergennes was far from impressed, which meant that when Oswald asked Vergennes for specific peace terms, the French foreign minister flatly refused to reveal anything. Not naturally inclined towards deviousness and not innately full of guile, Oswald may have been out of his league in the sophisticated, cunning drawing rooms of Versailles. He did understand the situation well enough, however, to remind Franklin on the trip back to Paris that American and French interests might not always align, especially if the French demands proved unreasonable. Franklin did not respond to this observation, but wrote to Shelburne asking that Oswald be officially credentialed as a representative of the British government.[110] Franklin liked working with Oswald and described him as a man who "seems to have nothing at heart but the good of mankind."[111] Not only was this the type of man with whom Franklin liked to deal, but it also indicated that Oswald's orientation would not be a major threat to American interests.

Undercut by both British parliamentary politics and the military realities created by the defeat at Yorktown, Oswald never had the opportunity to negotiate from a position of strength. By 1782, the British government was as deeply divided about parliamentary reform and economic reform as it was about negotiating a peace with the Americans.[112] On March 27, Charles Watson-Wentworth, the second Marquess of Rockingham, formed a weak ministry to replace that of Frederick North, who was a strong advocate for continuing the war. About the only thing Rockingham's ministers had in common was an opposition to the preceding government.[113] This internal discord can be seen in the rivalry between Shelburne as the Secretary of State for Home, Colonial, and Irish Affairs and Charles James Fox as the Secretary of State for Foreign Affairs. Shelburne was a monarchist, who believed the king should appoint his cabinet

---

[108] H. W. Brands, *The First American: The Life and Times of Benjamin Franklin* (New York: Doubleday, 2000), 601-602.
[109] Oswald, "Richard Oswald's Journal, April 18, 1782," 348-349.
[110] Schoenbrun, *Triumph in Paris*, 356.
[111] Benjamin Franklin quoted in John Cannon, *The Fox-North Coalition: The Crisis of the Constitution, 1782-4* (New York: Cambridge University Press, 1969), 16.
[112] Cannon, *The Fox-North Coalition*, 5-6.
[113] Frank W. Brecher, *Securing American Independence: John Jay and the French Alliance* (Westport, Connecticut: Praeger, 2003), 172.

ministers; Fox was a Parliamentarian, who believed in the collective power and responsibility of the cabinet.[114] Both men had an intense personal dislike for one another. Both men also had such a strong desire to direct the peace negotiations with the Americans that each sent his own representative to Paris. Shelburne named Oswald to negotiate with the Americans; to negotiate with the French, Fox appointed Thomas Grenville, a twenty-seven-year old aristocrat with no previous diplomatic experience. Despite clear instructions that Oswald and Grenville collaborate and communicate with one another regularly,[115] the two men failed to keep each other effectively informed.[116] This divided representation weakened Britain's negotiating strength significantly.

The American delegation had its own internal divisions, even if the disunity was less publicly obvious and made less political difference. In June 1781, the American Congress appointed five commissioners to negotiate a peace treaty with the British. Reflecting the non-federalist values of the Articles of Confederation,* the five commissioners represented the regional differences of the as-yet unrecognized nation: John Adams was to speak for New England, John Jay for New York, Benjamin Franklin for Pennsylvania, Thomas Jefferson for Virginia, and Henry Laurens for the Carolinas and Georgia. These five men were not all on good terms. Adams had lost his idolized respect for Franklin, while Franklin had grown tired of Adams' uncompromising righteousness and personal vanity.[117] Adams approached Jay with caution since the two men had disagreed significantly in sessions of the Continental Congress; Jay and Laurens had also quarreled in that setting.[118] Laurens was annoyed with Franklin over how little the Pennsylvanian had done to help while he was imprisoned in the Tower.[119] Fortunately for the Americans, however, only Franklin and Jay were in Paris through most of peace negotiations; this helped minimize the importance of personal tensions within the delegation.[120]

---

[114] John W. Derry, *Charles James Fox* (New York: St. Martin's Press, 1972), 151, 154, 157, 159.
[115] Lord Shelburne to Richard Oswald, May 21, 1782, *Memorials and Correspondence of Charles James Fox*, Volume IV, Lord John Russell (ed.) (New York, AMS Press, Inc., 1970), 201.
[116] Derry, *Charles James Fox*, 132.
[117] McCullough, *John Adams*, 197-198, 241-242.
[118] Walter Stahr, *John Jay: Founding Father* (New York: Hambledon and London, 2005), 102-103, 162.
[119] Laurens, "Journal and Narrative of Capture and Confinement in the Tower of London," 385.
[120] Jefferson refused to accept his appointment to the peace commission. This proved fortunate, for Jefferson's decision postponed his fierce disagreements with Adams due to their fundamental differences in attitude and approach. See, for example, Joyce Appleby, *Thomas Jefferson* (New York: Times Books/Henry Holt, 2003), 15-16; and Jon Meacham, *Thomas Jefferson: The Art of Power* (New York: Random House, 2012), 88-89, 103.

The negotiations began in May 1782, after Oswald returned to Paris with official authorization to represent the British government[121] and after Grenville arrived in France.[122] They proceeded through the summer and fall and centered upon seven issues: formal recognition of the United States as an independent nation; the new country's northern border; its western border; navigation rights on the Mississippi River; pre-war debts; compensation for the lost property of Loyalists; and fishing rights off Newfoundland. Progress was slow. Gradually, Franklin became increasingly willing to deal with the British independent of French oversight. This was a clear violation of Congress' instructions to defer to French leadership in the peace talks, but Franklin's shift in attitude allowed the conversations to progress.[123] This advance was partly offset by Jay's demand that, as a pre-condition for discussing any other terms, the British crown recognize American independence. He also took exception to the original language of Oswald's commission since it referred to the Thirteen States as Britain's "colonies and plantations" instead of as the "United States of America."[124] It wasn't until October 5 that Oswald presented his revised credentials to the American commissioners and finally satisfied Jay's objections.[125] Only then did the talks begin in earnest. When Adams arrived in Paris from the Dutch Republic at the end of October, he insisted that Britain uphold the American right to fish the Grand Banks and other customary fishing areas and recognize the American need to dry the fish on Canadian shores. The language surrounding this condition was so fraught with disagreement that this issue almost caused the talks to collapse.[126] In the end, Oswald agreed to give the Americans much of what they wanted because he and now-Prime Minister Shelburne realized that the best way to break the American-French alliance was to quickly secure the peace. In fact, Oswald had concluded as early as mid-July that Britain "ought to deal with [the Americans] tenderly, as supposed conciliated

---

[121] The Rockingham cabinet voted on April 23, 1782 to authorize Oswald. See Robinson, Jr., "Richard Oswald," 40.

[122] Grenville met Franklin for the first time on May 9, 1792. See "Benjamin Franklin's Peace Journal, May 9, 1782," *The Emerging Nation: A Documentary History of the Foreign Relations of the United States Under the Articles of Confederation, 1780-1789*, Mary A. Giunta (ed.) (Washington, DC: National Historical Publications and Records Commission, 1996), 376.

[123] Walter Isaacson, *Benjamin Franklin: An American Life* (New York: Simon & Schuster, 2003), 406.

[124] Brecher, *Securing American Independence*, 172.

[125] Isaacson, *Benjamin Franklin*, 409.

[126] "Richard Oswald to Thomas Townshend, November 30, 1782," *The Emerging Nation: A Documentary History of the Foreign Relations of the United States Under the Articles of Confederation, 1780-1789*, Mary A. Giunta (ed.) (Washington, DC: National Historical Publications and Records Commission, 1996), 695.

friends" because treating them harshly will only push them "into more close connection with [the French] court and our other enemies."[127] Oswald also believed that Atlantic trade would again thrive once it was unencumbered by war. He realized that, having lost the battles of Saratoga and Yorktown, the British should move promptly to make the most of the Atlantic's post-war economic opportunities.

On November 30, 1782, Franklin, Jay, Adams, and Laurens met Oswald in his suite at the Grand Hôtel Muscovite, not far from Saint-Germain-des-Prés, to sign the Preliminary Articles of Peace. The agreement set the longest borders of the United States at the Mississippi River and through the middle of the Great Lakes; ensured that the Mississippi River would remain open to navigation by both British and American citizens; granted Americans the right to fish the Grand Banks and the Gulf of St. Lawrence and to dry and cure fish in any unsettled areas in Nova Scotia and Labrador but not on the island of Newfoundland; assured both British and American creditors that they would not be impeded from collecting debts; made token promises about compensation of Loyalist property confiscated or destroyed during the war; provided for the release of prisoners by both sides; and called for the withdrawal of British troops "with all convenient speed & without causing any destruction or carrying away any Negros, or other property."[128]

The addition of the clause concerning the removal of Black slaves came in the final days of negotiation at the behest of Laurens. It came as a direct result of his pre-war business dealings with Oswald. In 1768, Oswald sold his rights to 5,340 acres in South Carolina to Laurens and John Lewis Gervais, a man Oswald had hired during the Seven Years' War to manage one of his German granaries. As part of the deal, Oswald loaned Gervais slaves, including some from his Florida property. At war's end, Gervais still owed Oswald for these slaves, but had no hope of repaying him since all of the slaves had run away during the war. Like many other slaves during the American Revolution, Gervais' slaves fled because the British promised Blacks their post-war freedom in exchange for their wartime assistance. By adding the "Negro clause" to the peace treaty, Laurens offered Oswald a way of recouping his loses.[129] This was the sordid underbelly of the

---

[127] "Richard Oswald to Lord Shelburne, July 12, 1782," *Memorials and Correspondence of Charles James Fox*, Volume IV, Lord John Russell (ed.) (New York: AMS Press, 1970), 247, 249.
[128] "Preliminary Articles of Peace between the United States and Great Britain, November 30, 1782," *The Emerging Nation: A Documentary History of the Foreign Relations of the United States Under the Articles of Confederation, 1780-1789*, Mary A. Giunta (ed.) (Washington, DC: National Historical Publications and Records Commission, 1996), 697-701.
[129] Robert Scott Davis, "Richard Oswald as 'An American': How a Frontier South Carolina Plantation Identifies the Anonymous Author of American Husbandry and a Forgotten Father of the United States," *Journal of Backcountry Studies*, Volume 8, Number 1 (Spring 2014), 19-34,

negotiations. Its inclusion in the final treaty meant that another one of the United States' foundational documents would be explicitly tainted with racial considerations.

The British reaction to the preliminary terms Oswald signed was overwhelmingly negative. A typical response was that of Lord Stormont in the House of Lords, who argued that Oswald had been outwitted by the Americans and that the resulting treaty was utterly one-sided as a result. For evidence, Stormont pointed to a particular clause in the preamble and wrote:

For in return for the manifold concessions on our part, not one has been made on theirs. In truth, the American commissioners had enriched the English dictionary with several new terms and phrases; reciprocal advantages, for instance, meant the advantage of one of the parties.[130]

Such barbs continued unabated through January and February 1783 and eventually resulted in both the collapse of Shelburne's government and Oswald's resignation as peace

Figure 8: James Gillray, "The Times, anno. 1783,"[detail], courtesy of the Library of Congress, 2004676762. The print shows the symbol of England, John Bull, throwing up his arms in despair as the devil flies away with a map labeled "America."

---

accessed January 19, 2020, http://libjournal.uncg.edu/jbc/article/view/935. When East Florida returned to Spanish control in 1784 as part of the Treaty of Paris, Oswald made arrangements for his slaves to be shipped to South Carolina, Georgia, or British Caribbean islands, where they could be resold. This too helped minimize his financial losses from the American Revolution. See Landers, *Black Society in Spanish Florida*, 159.

[130] Lord Stormont quoted in Cannon, *The Fox-North Coalition*, 52.

Figure 9: "The United States of America, According to the Treaty of Peace of 1784," map by John Russell, 1784?, courtesy of the Lionel Pincus and Princess Firyal Map Division, The New York Public Library, Map Div. 01-5254.

commissioner.[131] Oswald's replacement, David Hartley, tried to win additional concessions in subsequent months but was unable to make meaningful changes to the agreement. Franklin, Adams, Jay, and Hartley signed the final Treaty of Paris on September 3, 1783. Later that day, the British, French, and Spanish signed a separate agreement at Versailles, officially ending all hostilities.[132] That the Americans signed a different treaty meant that they violated the terms of their

---

[131] Cannon, *The Fox-North Coalition*, 58 and Schoenbrun, *Triumph in Paris*, 388. Shelburne offered his resignation February 24, 1783 and it became official on March 26.
[132] Stahr, *John Jay*, 179-183.

alliance with the French.¹³³ It also meant that Oswald's geopolitical assessment during his first week in France was correct: in the long run, American and British interests were better aligned than Franco-American ones.

Oswald demonstrated his faith in the Anglo-American future eighteen months after he had signed the preliminary agreement with the American commissioners. In late May 1784, he boarded a coach in London with his good friend Laurens and headed to Dover. He made the journey so that might see Jay one last time before Jay boarded his ship for New York.¹³⁴ As the men spent hours reminiscing over the negotiations and discussing the future of commerce and diplomacy in the Atlantic world, they affirmed their common roots and hope for a peaceful future that was not to be.¹³⁵

~

On November 6, 1784, eight years after Oswald died on his luxurious but not ostentatious Ayrshire estate in southwest Scotland, an anonymous abolitionist published a pamphlet in which a former Jamaican slave named Cushoo meets a friend of his former owner. During their conversation, Cushoo convinces the gentleman to stop consuming sugar and rum until the slave trade is abolished.¹³⁶ The clear lesson for the reader is that there are horrifying human consequences for enjoying sweetened tea and other foods made from cane sugar. It is the same lesson that Voltaire's Candide learns in Surinam, where he encounters a slave who has lost his right hand in a sugar factory and his left leg trying to escape the brutality of slavery.¹³⁷

Works like these fueled support for the abolition movement in the late eighteenth and early nineteenth centuries, but Oswald's heirs were not among those who joined the crusade. His wife Mary inherited all of his property on a life-rent basis, which meant that she received the benefits of Oswald's estate until

---

133 Brecher, *Securing American Independence*, 225.
134 Stahr, *John Jay*, 194. Benjamin Vaughan, who had also been involved in the peace negotiations at Shelburne's urging, was present for these conversations.
135 War between the United States and Great Britain resumed in 1812.
136 Anonymous, *No Rum! – No sugar! Or, The Voice of Blood, Being Half an Hour's Conversation between a Negro and an English Gentleman Showing the Horrible Nature of the Slave Trade and Pointing Out an Easy and Effectual Method of Terminating It by an Act of the People* (London: Printed for L. Wayland, 1792), 1-23.
137 Voltaire, *Candide or Optimism*, Henry Morley and Lauren Walsh (trans.) (New York: Barnes & Noble Classics, 2003), 76-77.

her death but could not distribute or dispose of the assets herself.[138] This meant little changed. Upon Mary's death in 1788, Oswald's nephews, John and Alexander Anderson, followed in their uncle's footsteps and embraced slaving as a profitable venture. When the Andersons inherited a five-ninths share in Bance Island, they purchased the remaining shares from the other owners. They then refurbished the island's facilities, which had fallen into ruin as a result of a French bombardment during the American Revolution. Once the retrofit was complete, the Andersons resumed the slave trade from Bance with the same energy their uncle had. They continued to ship large numbers of Africans across the Atlantic until 1800.[139] Like Oswald, the Andersons did not care to know about the details of the island's slave yard, where in 1791 Anna Falconbridge saw "between two and three hundred wretched victims, chained and parceled out in circles, just satisfying the cravings of nature from a trough of rice placed in the center of each circle."[140] Instead, like Oswald, the Andersons focused their attention on slave prices, overhead costs, mortality rates, and competition. Morality was not a significant concern. Like Oswald, the Andersons knew the right people and the right ways to influence public policy in times of crisis. As a member of Parliament, for example, John Anderson led the victorious charge in 1791 against a bill to prohibit British slave trading along a thousand-mile stretch of the West African coast, including Bance Island.[141] The Andersons also enjoyed their uncle's knack for impeccable timing, for they returned to the slave trade at a particularly lucrative time: between 1791 and 1800, British ships brought almost 400,000 slaves to the Americas and made an average profit of 13%.[142] As a result of their successes, the Anderson brothers did not terminate the Bance Island operation until 1811—four years after Parliament passed legislation outlawing the slave trade.[143] Clearly, Oswald had trained his nephews well in the art of business.

---

[138] "Correspondence of the Oswald family of Auchincruive, including Richard Oswald (1705-1784)," *Archives Hub*, accessed January 19, 2020, https://tinyurl.com/y5ky7t28. Mary Alexander Ramsay Oswald died December 6, 1788, four years and a month after her husband. Before she died, Mary sought to claim damages as a result of the Treaty of Paris' return of Florida to Spain. She claimed a loss of £9,298 10s. for the value of Mount Oswald but received only £3,921 5s. in the final settlement. See Wayne, *Sweet Cane*: 55-56.
[139] Hancock, *Citizens of the World*, 214-216.
[140] A. M. Falconbridge, *Narrative of Two Voyages to the River Sierra Leone during the Years 1791-1793* (London: Frank Cass & Co. Ltd, 1967), 32.
[141] Rawley, *London, Metropolis of the Slave Trade*, 140.
[142] Thomas, *The Slave Trade*, 541.
[143] Hancock, *Citizens of the World*, 216.

Glossary:

Articles of Confederation: A form of American government from 1781-1789 which was designed to maintain the power of the individual states and keep the central government weak. The system provided for each state having one vote in Congress.

The Enlightenment: An intellectual movement that prized reason. It dominated European thought in the eighteenth century.

Hogshead: A volume measurement defined by a large cask or barrel; while there was some variety due to differences in the diameters of barrels, a hogshead was typically 63 gallons.

Indentured Servants: In exchange for transportation to the British colonies in North America, these people were subject to a five to seven-year labor contract. Upon the completion of their contract, indentured servants became free.

Mercantilism: An economic theory that holds that careful regulation, instead of free trade, is the best way to maximize profits and growth for one nation while simultaneously taking away profits from competing countries.

Physiocrats: The eighteenth-century economic and political theorists who saw agriculture was the basis of the economy, opposed mercantilism*, and advocated for free trade within certain limitations.

WAR OF THE AUSTRIAN SUCCESSION (1740-1748): In October 1740, Holy Roman Emperor and Habsburg monarch Charles VI died without a male heir. His will designated his eldest daughter, Maria Theresa (1717-1780), as sovereign of Austria, Bohemia, Croatia, Galicia, Hungary, Transylvania, and other territories. This inheritance was challenged by Bavaria, France, and Prussia because it contradicted a legal tradition established by Clovis, King of the Franks (466-511 CE), that excluded women from inheriting property. The eight-year war resulted in Maria Theresa retaining her throne but losing the key province of Silesia to Prussia.

Suggested Reading:

Abbott, Elizabeth. *Sugar: A Bittersweet History*. New York: Duckworth Overlook, 2009.
Baptist, Edward E. *Creating an Old South: Middle Florida's Plantation Frontier Before the Civil War*. Chapel Hill: University of North Carolina Press, 2002.
Burnard, Trevor. *Planters, Merchants, and Slaves: Plantation Societies in British America, 1650-1820*. Chicago, Illinois: University of Chicago Press, 2015.
Diouf, Sylviane A. *Slavery's Exiles: The Story of the American Maroons*. New York: New York University Press, 2014.
Hahn, Barbara. *Making Tobacco Bright: Creating an American Commodity, 1617-1937*. Baltimore, Maryland: The Johns Hopkins Press, 2011.
Isaacson, Walter. *Benjamin Franklin: An American Life*. New York: Simon & Schuster, 2003.
Parker, Matthew. *The Sugar Barons: Family, Corruption, Empire and War in the West Indies*. New York: Walker and Company, 2011.
Stahr, Walter. *John Jay: Founding Father*. New York: Hambledon and London, 2005.
Stobart, Jon. *Sugar and Spice: Grocers and Groceries in Provincial England 1650-1830*. Oxford, U.K.: Oxford University Press, 2013.
Stubbs, Tristan. *Masters of Violence: The Plantation Overseers of Eighteenth-Century Virginia, South Carolina, and Georgia*. Columbia, South Carolina: University of South Carolina Press, 2018.
White, Jerry. *London in the 18th Century: A Great and Monstrous Thing*. London: Vintage Books, 2013.
Williams, Ian. *Rum: A Social and Sociable History*. New York: Nation Books, 2005.

www.ingramcontent.com/pod-product-compliance
Lightning Source LLC
Chambersburg PA
CBHW050320220526
45465CB00005B/2062